RHS

Ultimate Sticker Book
GARDEN POND

DK | Penguin Random House

With thanks to Ben Hoare for first edition
text on pages 4–5 and 8–11.

Editor Abi Maxwell
Assistant Editor Soumya Rampal
US Senior Editor Shannon Beatty
Project Art Editor Bhagyashree Nayak
Assistant Art Editor Mansi Dwivedi
Design Assistant Sif Nørskov
Illustrator Rachael Hare
Deputy Managing Editor Roohi Sehgal
Managing Editors Monica Saigal, Penny Smith
Managing Art Editor Ivy Sengupta
DTP Designers Sachin Gupta, Nand Kishor Acharya
Project Picture Researcher Rituraj Singh
Picture Research Administrator Vagisha Pushp
Senior Jacket Designer Rashika Kachroo
Production Editor Becky Fallowfield
Senior Production Controller Ben Radley
Delhi Creative Head Malavika Talukder
Art Director Mabel Chan
Publisher Francesca Young
Managing Director Sarah Larter

Royal Horticultural Society
Consultant Helen Bostock
Editor Simon Maughan
Books Publishing Manager Helen Griffin
Head of Editorial Tom Howard

This American edition, 2024
Previously published as
Ultimate Sticker Book: RHS Garden Flowers (2006)
by DK Publishing,
a division of Penguin Random House LLC
1745 Broadway, 20th Floor, New York, NY 10019
in association with The Royal Horticultural Society

Copyright © 2006, 2024 Dorling Kindersley Limited
24 25 26 27 28 10 9 8 7 6 5 4 3 2 1
001–341094–May/2024

A catalog record for this book is available
from the Library of Congress.
ISBN: 978-0-7440-9961-4

DK books are available at special discounts when
purchased in bulk for sales promotions, premiums,
fund-raising, or educational use. For details, contact:
DK Publishing Special Markets, 1745 Broadway,
20th Floor, New York, NY 10019
SpecialSales@dk.com

Printed and bound in China

www.dk.com

Activities

Here are the six different types of activities
that you will find inside this book. Have fun!

Find it! Hunt for the correct stickers that fit the blank spaces.

Follow! Follow the trail and put the correct stickers on the pages.

Match it! Match the correct sticker with each picture to complete the images.

Make it! Put stickers on the pages to create your own scene.

Fit it! Find the stickers that fit the blank spaces and complete the big picture.

Guess it! Try the fun sticker quiz. All the answers are in the book!

Acknowledgments

Dorling Kindersley would like to thank Kritika Gupta for editorial support in the preparation of this book.
The publisher would like to thank the following for their kind permission to reproduce their photographs:
(Key: a=above; b=below/bottom; c=center; f=far; l=leftr=right; t=top)

1 Alamy Stock Photo: Brian Bevan (cla/wasps); Alec Scaresbrook (bc/Leaf). **Dorling Kindersley:** RHS Wisley / Mark Winwood (bc). **Dreamstime.com:** Maxim Karlione (cla). **Getty Images:** Ullstein Bild (cra). **Getty Images / iStock:** Drakuliren (tr). **2 Alamy Stock Photo:** Panther Media GmbH (cla). **Dreamstime.com:** Shuen Ho Wang (cr); Photka (cr/Rocks). **Getty Images / iStock:** Henrik_L (c). **2–13 Dreamstime.com:** Aga7ta (Texture). **2–3 Alamy Stock Photo:** Colin Varndell (bc). **Dreamstime.com:** Melanie Martin (bc/Pond); Les Palenik (ca); Ovydyborets (bc/stones). **3 Alamy Stock Photo:** Ambling Images (br/Grass); Alec Scaresbrook (cb). **Dreamstime.com:** Allexxandar (tr); Tongchuwit (clb); Beebrain (br). **Getty Images / iStock:** Drakuliren (tr/swallows). **4 123RF.com:** Portokalis (cla). **Getty Images:** Ullstein Bild (tr). **Getty Images / iStock:** Michel Viard (bl). **5 Alamy Stock Photo:** Sabena Jane Blackbird (tr); Juniors Bildarchiv Gmbh / Juniors@Wildlife (cl); Ian West (tl). **Getty Images / iStock:** Igorbondarenko (crb). **6–7 Alamy Stock Photo:** Pcpexclusive. **8 Alamy Stock Photo:** imageBROKER / Dave Pressland (br/Boatman); Nature Picture Library / Dale Sutton / 2020VISION (ca); Kay Roxby (cb). **Dreamstime.com:** Ernest Cooper (br). **9 Alamy Stock Photo:** Blickwinkel / F. Hecker (cb). **Dreamstime.com:** Beebrain (tr); Rostislav Stefanek (tl); Photka (tr/Rocks); Rudmer Zwerver (cl). **Shutterstock.com:** Vitalii Hulai (bc). **10 Alamy Stock Photo:** Ulrike Leone (c); Julian Popov (bl). **Shutterstock.com:** Ger Bosma Photos (cla); Peter Turner Photography (cla/Pond). **11 Alamy Stock Photo:** Zoonar / Ewald Fr (ca). **Dreamstime.com:** Mikelane45 (clb); Ondej Prosick (crb). **12 Alamy Stock Photo:** Alec Scaresbrook (cla). **Dreamstime.com:** Happy Job (c). **13 Dreamstime.com:** Ahmet Yamak (tc). **Getty Images / iStock:** E+ / SolStock (cra). **14–15 Alamy Stock Photo:** A Garden. **16 123RF.com:** Portokalis (bl). **Alamy Stock Photo:** Blickwinkel / F. Hecker (clb); Pcpexclusive (br). **Dreamstime.com:** Aga7ta (texture); Carlosphotos (ca); Tongchuwit (cla); Ulrike Leone (cra/Mayfly); Rostislav Stefanek (clb). **Getty Images:** Ullstein Bild (tl). **Getty Images / iStock:** FedBul (crb); Henrik_L (cla). **Shutterstock.com:** Patrick C Fox (tr). **18 Alamy Stock Photo:** David Sewell (ca). **Dorling Kindersley:** RHS Wisley / Mark Winwood (fbl/X2). **Dreamstime.com:** Allexxandar (bl/X2); Carlosphotos (cla); Tongchuwit (cra); Saccobent (c); O2beat (cl, fbr/X2); Rudmer Zwerver (clb, br/X2). **Getty Images / iStock:** Drakuliren (cb/X2). **Shutterstock.com:** Nicholas Toh (cra/Smail). **19 123RF.com:** Portokalis (c, fbr/Bulrush X2). **Alamy Stock Photo:** Sabena Jane Blackbird (cla); Juniors Bildarchiv Gmbh / Juniors@Wildlife (cra, bl/X2); Ian West (fbl/Water Violet X2, cra/Water Violet, tl). **Getty Images:** Ullstein Bild (cl, fbr/X2). **Getty Images / iStock:** Igorbondarenko (ca, br/X2); Michel Viard (cr, fbl/X2). **22 Alamy Stock Photo:** Pcpexclusive (ca/X4, fbl/X2); Wildlife Gmbh (cl). **Dreamstime.com:** Isselee (cla). **Science Photo Library:** Simon Booth (crb, fbr/X2). **23 Alamy Stock Photo:** Blickwinkel / F. Hecker (tr); imageBROKER.com GmbH & Co. KG / Dave Pressland (tl, clb/X2); Papilio / Robert Pickett (cra, fbr/X2); Nature Picture Library / Dale Sutton / 2020VISION (cr, crb/X2); DP Wildlife Invertebrates (cl). **Dreamstime.com:** Kikkerdirk / Dirk Ercken (fbl/X2); Rudmer Zwerver (tc/amhibian); Rostislav Stefanek (ca, br/X2); Viter8 (bl/X2). **Shutterstock.com:** Patrick C Fox (c). **26 Alamy Stock Photo:** Brian Bevan (ca/wasps, fcrb/X2); Blickwinkel / Layer (ca); INSADCO GmbH / McPHOTO / SHU (cra); Frances Browne (cra/Dragonfly); Imagemore Co., Ltd. (cr, crb/X2). **Dreamstime.com:** Anders93 (br/X2); Ondej Prosick (ca); Mikelane45 (ca/chaser, fbr/X2); Julian Popov (cl, fbr/X2); Ulrike Leone (c, fbl/X2); Valentino2 (fclb/Toad X2). **Getty images / iStock:** JanMiko (fcrb/Gerris X2). **Shutterstock.com:** Ger Bosma Photos (ca). **27 Alamy Stock Photo:** Alex Fieldhouse (cla, bl/X2). **Dreamstime.com:** Maxim Karlione (cra); Yrastocs (ca, br/X2); Ahmet Yamak (tr). **Getty Images / iStock:** FedBul (c). **30 Alamy Stock Photo:** Agami Photo Agency / Wil Leurs (cr); Nature in Stock / Jan van Arkel (cla); Nature Photographers Ltd / Paul R. Sterry (cra); Blickwinkel / E. Teister (cra/leaf); Alessandro Mancini (c); Blickwinkel / W. Willner (cr/caddisfly); Gillian Pullinger (bl/ramp); Sabena Jane Blackbird (cla). **Dreamstime.com:** Steven Cukrov (tc/Garden Snail); Wirestock (tl, tr); Yuryz (cl); Lostafichuk (cl); Rudmer Zwerver (cb/Frog); Karin59 (br). **Getty Images / iStock:** Skymoon13 (br/Tanacetum vulgare). **Shutterstock.com:** Taniaaraujo (bl); Rudmer Zwerver (tc/Snail). **31 123RF.com:** Portokalis (fcrb/Bulrush X2). **Alamy Stock Photo:** Brian Bevan (crb/Wasps X2); Juniors Bildarchiv Gmbh / Juniors@Wildlife (cl/X2); Sabena Jane Blackbird (br/X2 Mentha aquatica). **Dorling Kindersley:** RHS Wisley / Mark Winwood (cl/Nymphaea X2). **Dreamstime.com:** Ernest Cooper (fcrb/X2); O2beat (fcr/X2); Rudmer Zwerver (fclb/Frog X2); Yrastocs (bl/X2); Julian Popov (br/X2). **Getty Images / iStock:** Igorbondarenko (fclb/Butomus umbellatus X2). **Shutterstock.com:** Nicholas Toh (cl/Snail X2).

Cover images: *Front:* **123RF.com:** Portokalis bl, Leszek Starybrat / viejo cr; **Alamy Stock Photo:** Brian Bevan crb/ (wasp), INSADCO GmbH / McPHOTO / SHU clb; **Dorling Kindersley:** RHS Wisley / Mark Winwood cb; **Dreamstime.com:** Isselee cl, bc, Roman Ivaschenko bc/ (leaf), Alain Michaud tl, Ondej Prosick bl/ (Heron), Wirestock crb, Rudmer Zwerver bc/ (Frog); **Getty Images:** Ullstein Bild cla; **Getty Images / iStock:** Drakuliren tr, Skymoon13 ftr; *Back:* **123RF.com:** Leszek Starybrat / viejo cra/ (lily). **Alamy Stock Photo:** Blickwinkel / Layer crb, Blickwinkel / W. Willner tl, Alec Scaresbrook br; **Dreamstime.com:** Isselee cra, Roman Ivaschenko ftr, Sayhmog bl, Rudmer Zwerver tr

All other images © Dorling Kindersley

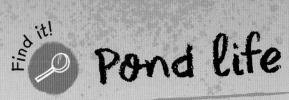 **Find it!**

Pond life

Ponds are home to many animals, including frogs, fish, and creepy-crawlies, that live in or around water. Many birds also visit ponds to eat pond plants or creepy-crawlies, drink water, or have a bath.

Butterfly

Creepy-crawlies
Many different kinds of creepy-crawly can be found in a pond. Some live underwater, while others swim in it or walk on the surface. The great diving beetle dives deep, but comes up for air. Adult dragonflies hunt for food in the air, but their young live underwater.

Dragonfly

Great diving beetle

Fish
Fish add color and movement to the pond. They feed on a wide range of pond animals, including mosquito larvae and tadpoles. Goldfish and koi carp are the most common fish that can be seen in garden ponds, though a wildlife pond is better without fish because they predate on other wildlife.

Goldfish

Koi carp

Mallard

Birds

Some birds come to ponds in search of food. Swallows swoop down to catch creepy-crawlies and collect mud for their nests. Mallards visit ponds to feed on plants and small animals. Many other birds make their way to ponds to bathe and drink water.

Swallows

Other visitors

Grass snakes, also called water snakes, swim in ponds to hunt for food. The ramshorn snail feeds on the algae that grows in ponds.

Grass snake

Amphibians

Amphibians live both in and out of the pond. Frogs jump into the water to lay their eggs, called spawn. Newts use their tails to dart forward to catch creepy-crawlies.

Frog

Ramshorn snail

Newt

Pond plants

Different types of plant live in ponds. Some grow underwater, some float on the surface, and others prefer the damp soil beside the pond. These plants provide food, shelter, and nesting sites for pond animals.

Marsh marigold
Another name for this bright plant is kingcup. In the wild, it is found beside streams and in water meadows.

Reed mace
This tall plant grows thick brown tubes that look a little like sausages. These are actually its flowers and seedheads! The plant is also known as cat's-tail.

The brown tubes of reed mace, also known as pokers, are filled with thousands of seeds.

"Red Emperor" Monkey flower
This plant is popular for its trumpet-shaped flowers that are scarlet red in color. Its leaves are oval-shaped and light green, with pointy edges.

Water violet

This is an underwater plant with pale lilac flowers. Its light green foliage can be seen both on and under the surface of the water. This plant keeps the pond well-oxygenated.

Water mint

The leaves of water mint have a wonderful smell. They are used to perfume shampoo, bubble bath, and other beauty products.

Water shamrock

The water shamrock's leaves are shiny and green. They have four parts and make interesting patterns on the water's surface.

Flowering rush

This plant likes the muddy edges of ponds and can grow up to 5 ft (1.5 m) tall. It has pretty, pink flowers in summer.

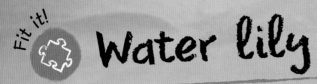

Water lily

You can easily spot a water lily by its rounded leaf pads that float on the water. Frogs and creepy-crawlies use them as islands to rest on. There are about 50 wild species of water lilies. With their glossy leaves and bright flowers, water lilies are an attractive addition to garden ponds.

White water lily

The white water lily has circular, waxy leaves. Its white flowers bloom in mid-to-late summer. This plant grows up to 5 ft (1.5 m). Fish hide underneath its big leaves to protect themselves from predatory birds.

A spread of lily pads allows less sunlight to enter the pond, providing shade to the pond animals and discouraging the growth of algae.

The white flowers bloom in the morning and close up again by late afternoon. These flowers attract beetles who stay the night inside the closed-up flowers and get released at dawn.

The Amazon water lily is known to have one of the largest leaves of any plant. A single plant can grow up to 50 huge leaves. Each leaf may be more than 5 ft (1.5 m) wide.

Life cycle of a frog

While frogs like to rest on lily pads, they usually pick a sunny, open spot in the water to lay their eggs.

A female frog lays many frog spawn in water.

Tadpoles hatch from the eggs. They have tails and live in water.

Over time, tadpoles grow into froglets. Their tails shrink and legs become stubby.

Finally, the froglets grow into adult frogs. They can live both in and out of the water.

Underwater creatures

Beneath the surface, garden ponds are full of life. Snails, creepy-crawlies, tadpoles, and frogs all thrive underwater. Many people keep fish in their pond, but the fish eat lots of other water animals. This means that ponds with fish usually have less wildlife.

Common frog

The common frog feeds on worms, spiders, slugs, flies, and many other invertebrates that it catches with its long, sticky tongue. It rests by day and hunts at night. In spring, frogs head for ponds to breed.

Frog spawn

In spring, a female frog lays jellylike eggs, called frog spawn. The black "dot" in the middle of each egg turns into a tadpole.

Water boatman

The water boatman swims upside down using its hairy back legs as paddles. It eats tadpoles and pond creepy-crawlies.

Stickleback

The stickleback is named for the sharp spines on its back. The fish is mottled brownish-green, except in the breeding season, when the male's belly turns red.

Great pond snail

This snail can often be found stuck to the sides of the pond. It grazes on slimy green pondweed, which helps to keep the water clean. It is also a great source of food for birds.

Smooth newt

A common sight near ponds, the smooth newt can be gray or brown in color. It eats beetles, small slugs, snails, and sometimes even frog spawn and tadpoles.

Water scorpion

This creepy-crawly uses its pincerlike front legs to grab its prey. If you try to catch one, it can give a painful nip.

Water hog-louse

Mostly found at the bottom of a pond, this small creepy-crawly absorbs oxygen through its shell. It is often considered a pond cleaner since it eats the remains of dead plants.

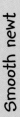

Fit it!

Life at the surface

Ponds are a magnet for garden wildlife. Birds and mammals visit ponds for a variety of different reasons. Some animals need ponds to breed and lay their eggs in the water.

Wasp

Creepy-crawlies, such as wasps, hornets, and bees, all visit the shallow pond margins or damp surfaces of pond plants to have a drink.

Common toad

Toads come to ponds to breed and lay their eggs. Male toads call females to the pond with loud croaking.

Mayfly

Young mayflies live underwater for up to two or three years. In spring and summer, adult mayflies emerge from the water and live for just a few days.

Blue-tailed damselfly

Search for these dameselflies at the edges of ponds. They have a partially blue body with see-through wings.

Wood pigeon

Pigeons eat dry food such as seeds so they need to drink a lot. They suck water up through their beak as if using a straw.

Common darter dragonfly

Dragonflies perch on plants to watch for creepy-crawlies flying past, and then chase after them. The dragonflies then return to the same perch to enjoy their meal.

The common darter dragonfly gets its name from the way it darts toward prey in short, fast flights.

Pond skater

Pond skaters use the sensitive hairs on their legs to detect the movement of prey. They then hop across the surface of the water, and eat creepy-crawlies that have fallen in.

Gray heron

Ponds with fish attract herons. These birds stay perfectly still until a fish comes into range and then grab it in their daggerlike bills.

Broad-bodied chaser

Like all dragonflies, chasers have four big wings and are fast, graceful fliers. Adult males are powder blue in color, while females are brown.

START

Garden pond

Use gently!

Collect specimens

Dip the net

Observe specimens

⚠️

Always go pond dipping with an adult.

Transfer carefully

Follow!

Pond dipping

Pond dipping is a fun way to explore the fascinating world of garden ponds. This watery world is home to many wonderful animals and plants. Find a clean pond and choose a safe area near the water's edge where you can start pond dipping. Follow the trail, enjoy the activity, and make sure to return any creatures to the pond when you finish.

Take pictures

Record observations

Zoom in for close-up pictures!

FINISH

Leaving the jar in a sunny spot will overheat the creatures. So, return them to the same part of the pond when finished.

Use a magnifying glass

Look closely!

Remember to wash your hands and nets after you have finished the activity.

Let's get going!

Reward yourself with a sticker every time you complete a step.

Dip the net

Use a dip net to catch different creatures. Sweep it through the water to collect specimens.

Collect specimens

Turn the dip net inside out and release the creatures into a jar half-filled with pond water.

Observe specimens

Half-fill a second jar with pond water. Gently transfer the creatures one by one into this jar for observation.

Use a magnifying glass

Observe small specimens by using a handheld magnifying glass.

Record observations

Make notes of what you observe in your notebook. You can also sketch some interesting creatures.

Take pictures

You can even take pictures of the specimens, add labels, and stick them in your notebook.

Design your garden pond

Are you ready to create your own garden pond? You can make it colorful by choosing stickers of your favorite plants, such as irises, pondweed, water lilies, water mint, marsh marigolds, and more! You can also add stickers of creepy-crawlies and animals to bring your pond to life.

1. Which pond plant is also called kingcup?

2. What are the eggs of a frog called?

3. Which beetle can dive deep into ponds, but has to come up for air?

4. Name the most common fish that can be seen in garden ponds.

Guess it!

Sticker quiz

Reward yourself with a frog sticker for each question you answer correctly.

5. Which fish is named for the sharp spines on its back?

6. Mayflies live underwater their entire lives. True or false?

7. What does the water scorpion use to grab its prey?

8. What should be used to catch different creatures while pond dipping?

9. Which plant has thick brown tubes, that look a little like sausages?

10. White water lilies bloom in mid-to-late summer. True or False?

1. Marsh marigold 2. Frog spawn 3. Great diving beetle 4. Koi carp and goldfish 5. Stickleback 6. False 7. Pincerlike front legs 8. Dip net 9. Reed mace 10. True